COLLECTIVE WORSHIP IN THE PRIMARY SCHOOL

Series Editor: Terence Cop'

CELEBRATING OUR ENVIRONMENT

by
Elizabeth Ashton

SOUTHGATE

First published 1994 by Southgate Publishers Ltd

Southgate Publishers Ltd
Glebe House, Church Street, Crediton, Devon EX17 2AF

Illustrations by Michael Lye

Printed and bound in Great Britain by Short Run Press Ltd, Exeter, Devon

British Library Cataloguing in Publication Data.
A CIP catalogue record for this book is available from the British Library.

ISBN 1-85741-067-X

ACKNOWLEDGEMENTS

Mrs Janet White, Head Teacher, Dipton Collierly Primary School, Co. Durham, who provided the poem written by one of her pupils which is printed on page 40.

Key to Section symbols in text:

REFLECT   STORY   CONSIDER   PRAY   HYMN and MUSIC

CONTENTS

INTRODUCTION
Collective Worship in the Primary School

THE LAW

The 1988 Education Reform Act required worship in schools. Although more flexible than the 1944 Act, in that it could be held at any time of the school day and in any grouping, worship remained a daily requirement. Parents retained the legal right to withdraw their children from school worship; teachers retained the legal right to withdraw themselves!

It was now 'collective worship' – never 'assembly' in the law. 'Collective' was held to mean that sensitivity had been shown to the real situation in schools: that in the assembly for worship there are all sorts of faiths and families, beliefs and unbeliefs, among the staff and pupils alike: a collection of pupils, not a corporate body of believers. Since the Act, DFE Circular 1/94 has added detail by way of advice.

Among religious communities, parents and teachers, the national debate continues, but it is not the purpose of this series to join in.

THIS SERIES

This series aims to provide teachers with practical help. In schools, alongside the legal requirements is a continuing need to provide interesting, sensitive material that combines good education with concern for the integrity of pupils and teachers. The writers have therefore tried to relate their units to the National Curriculum, to offer options to teachers, and to avoid any arbitrary suggestions for worship. So while the hard-pressed teacher can just pick up the book and use it, spending time in adaptation to their particular school worship will add to its quality.

The suggested acts of worship comply with the legal requirement for 'broadly Christian'. The amount of material from faiths other than Christianity varies, according to the theme of the book and its writer's choice. Detailed treatment of major faiths, including Christianity, must be left to RE. Collective worship is not a mass RE lesson in the hall but an activity required to be separate by law, educational principle and common sense! Religious and non-religious teachers alike will agree that it must not be an attempt to convert the captive children. But if it helps them to be more reflective, to see worth in people and things, then it cannot be said to be time wasted and it cannot be said to be divisive.

A note on God!   'God' is a name given by some people to a mysterious living reality and by others to a disputed idea they can't accept or aren't sure about. Not to use the word with children is to censor their experience as surely as if we try to indoctrinate them into belief in God. For millions of adults God is real, whether we personally agree with them or not. So what do we do? We can use the word anyway, on the grounds that it is real to many children. Or we could say, 'Some people believe that God ...' and leave the debate about God until the children are older.

Terence Copley

CELEBRATING OUR ENVIRONMENT

This book provides material for collective worship for primary school teachers. The material is presented in separate units which are complete in themselves to allow for convenient use but are intended to be flexible; they may be adapted to particular circumstances.

The book addresses the requirements of the Education (Reform) Act, 1988 and circular 1/94, 'Schools and Collective Worship', in that worship should be 'broadly Christian', with emphasis on similarities of belief and the symbols which are used in the expression of belief.

FOCUS

The focus of the material falls mainly into the following areas:

- Teaching children about environmental and conservation issues which are important in today's world.

- Linking the world of wildlife and the environment with spiritual and religious responsibility.

- Introducing children to the nature of religious symbolism, particularly symbols from the natural world.

- Providing opportunities and ideas for stimulating young children's feelings of awe and wonder concerning the natural world.

- Refining the concept of creation, with its implications of a creator – God, Allah, Brahman, YHWH, for example.

HOW TO USE THIS BOOK

- Each unit is complete in itself. It is also linked specifically to other units and generally to the focus of the whole volume.

- References to other books and useful addresses are provided on page 62.

- All resources needed for each unit are listed with the unit and some useful drawings needed for reference are included.

- Teachers are encouraged to relate the contents to current National Curriculum Attainment Targets.

- Most of the units have been designed to involve children and it is intended that further classroom work will develop from the units.

FLOWER SIGNS

Purpose   To show how flowers have become symbols for humans.

Resources   Pictures or examples of daffodil, rose, thistle, shamrock (or clover leaf); picture of Tudor Rose; Remembrance Day red poppy.

INTRODUCTION

Show the children pictures or real flowers and point out how different each flower is. Ask the younger children to show the differences; for example, size, colour, shape of flower and of leaves, time in bloom, perfume. Invite some children to feel the prickles of the thistle.

CONSIDER

Flowers are sometimes chosen by people as symbols, to stand for something that is important. Ask the children if they can think of any object that stands for something else, such as badges or uniforms.

Tell the children about the national emblems of the British Isles. Ask if anyone knows which flower stands for each country. The children may need reminding which countries make up the British Isles.

- *Rose (England)*   Show a picture of the Tudor Rose, which was made up of King Henry VII's family sign, the red rose, and the white rose that was the family sign of his wife, Elizabeth of York.

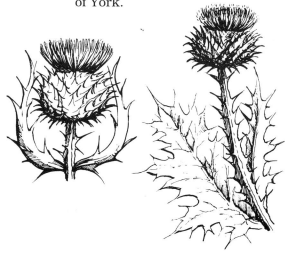

- *Thistle (Scotland)*   Show a thistle; point out its prickles. It was chosen as the sign of Scotland because of a legend about some Scottish soldiers who were attacked one night when asleep in their camp. Their enemies crept up barefoot, to take the soldiers by surprise, but they did not see the prickly thistles and stood on them. Their cries of pain woke the Scots who fought them off.

- *Shamrock (Ireland)* St Patrick was the first person to teach the Irish about Christianity. He taught people how Christians think of God in three different ways, as Father, Son and Holy Ghost. This was difficult to understand, so St Patrick used the three-leaved shamrock as a symbol to explain how something can be in three parts and yet still continue to be one thing.

- *Daffodil (Wales)* St David was a monk who lived in medieval times and was loved by the Welsh people. He became their special saint. His life is celebrated on St David's Day, 1st March. Can anyone think why the Welsh people chose the daffodil for their emblem? (It is in bloom on St David's Day in most parts of Wales.)

STORY

The red poppy is a symbol of remembrance (*ask some children to explain this*). During the First World War, the green fields of France and Belgium disappeared beneath the mud, the trenches and the scars of battle. When the fighting stopped, people were amazed to see poppies blooming where millions of soldiers had died.

The red petals matched the soldiers' blood, so the poppy was adopted as a symbol of the courage of the men and women who died fighting for the freedom of their country. That is why poppies are worn every year around the time of Remembrance Sunday (the Sunday nearest to 11th November), when we remember those who have died in war.

The seeds of the poppy are able to lie in the ground for hundreds of years without either growing or dying. They lie dormant, or asleep. But as soon as the ground is disturbed, as it was on the battlefields of Flanders, the seeds come back to life and begin to grow.

HYMN

Invite the children to join in singing the hymn, *Think of a World Without Any Flowers* (BBC hymn-book, *Come and Praise 1*).

PRAY

Invite the children to reflect.

Thank you for the gift of flowers, which cheer up the world
and give support for our ideas.

TREES ALL AROUND

Purpose   To provide examples of how the mysterious life of trees has become a symbol for human ideas about our own life.

Resources   Pictures of leaves; children's paintings or rubbings of leaves; sketches of skeleton outlines of trees. A sketch of fan vaulting from a church ceiling (e.g. St George's Chapel, Windsor). A picture of a laurel wreath, or samples of laurel leaves. An outline of the Jesse window from Durham Cathedral. A picture of a Christian cross.

INTRODUCTION

Show the children a sketch of the Jesse window. Can anyone work out from where the builders got their idea and why they did so? (The shape of a tree; it represents the idea of a family tree, branching out as the family grows.)

CONSIDER

- Trees have been very important to human beings throughout the ages. The branches of trees meeting overhead in a wood, or across a country lane, probably gave architects the idea for the decoration of church ceilings. (*Show the picture of fan vaulting.*)

- A tree was used to make the cross on which Jesus was crucified. The cross is a sign to Christian people of everlasting life. (*Show a picture of the Christian cross.*)

STORY

An old story from Greece tells how the laurel tree saved Daphne, who was wandering through the woods one day when the god Apollo saw her. He fell in love with her instantly and ran towards her, telling her how much he cared for her. Daphne was terrified and fled from him, through the woods. She was a fast runner but Apollo was faster. In terror, she cried out to her father, the god of the river, to save her.

An extraordinary thing happened. As Apollo caught up with her and threw his arms around her, he found he was touching the bark of a tree. Daphne's legs had become the trunk of a laurel tree and her arms and fingers were the branches and leaves. Apollo drew back in amazement. The laurel tree swayed gently in the breeze, its shining green leaves beautiful in the sunshine.

Laurel became a sign of triumph, because of Daphne's triumph over the pursuit by Apollo. The Romans made crowns of laurel leaves for their Emperors and others as a sign of victory. The laurel is still a popular shrub in gardens.

REFLECT

For many people trees are mysterious and exciting. Invite the children to read these lines from Hindu scripture:

Child 1   Whoever stays in the forest at evening: you think you see cows grazing;
Child 2   You think you see a house;
Child 3   You think a cart is rumbling.
(From the *Rig Veda*, Hindu Sacred Writings, Penguin, 1981, p.242)

PRAY

Let a child read this prayer, stressing each word in italics and pausing for emphasis where marked (–).

We ask for your help, God, in
noticing – the beauty of trees;
hearing – the sound of wind among branches;
marvelling – at shape, height and variety;
using – tree patterns to enrich our own thoughts.

HYMN

A suitable hymn might be: *As Jacob With Travel* (*Worship Songs, Ancient and Modern*, Canterbury Press, 1992).

FROM SEED TO TREE

Purpose   To tell the parable of the mustard seed, showing the children how stories can be used to explore meaning.

Resources   A few packets of flower seeds, both garden and wild. A picture of a mustard tree.

INTRODUCTION

Have you ever noticed that a plant will grow out of a tiny crack in the pavement or even on rooftops? (*Ask the children for examples they have seen.*) This is one of the wonderful things about nature. Seeds spread and grow in all sorts of places.

Show the children the packets of flower seeds. Ask some children to open them and tell the others what the seeds are like.

Has anyone ever seen a tiny seedling start to grow? Some people think that a miracle of nature is the way in which huge plants, like trees, begin their lives as tiny seedlings.

Here is a story about a man who once tried to get rid of all the flowers in his garden.

STORY

Jesus used a seed to try to explain what the Kingdom of Heaven is like. He spoke about the seed of the mustard plant. Everyone who listened to him knew about this seed because it was very common in their country, rather like the daisy in this country. Jesus reminded everyone that the mustard seed was probably one of the smallest seeds in existence, even smaller than a grain of sand.

When the seed began to grow, it seemed as though it would never stop. It grew into an enormous tree with huge, strong branches where the birds could rest.

Jesus taught the people that the Kingdom of Heaven is like that mustard seed. It begins from something very small but spreads very quickly.

REFLECT AND PRAY

Invite the children to think in their own way about the story. After a few moments introduce this prayer:

Just as there is scent in a flower
And reflection in a mirror,
So God is in you;
Find him in your heart.
(From the Guru Granth Sahib)

HYMN

He Made Me (BBC hymn-book, *Come and Praise 1*).

A WORLD FOR ANIMALS

Purpose   To introduce the idea that animals enrich the lives of humans and to tell the children the story of Ganesha.

Resources   Pictures of animals, preferably poster-size; if possible, pictures of endangered species such as the elephant and rhino. Any paintings or drawings done by the children could be displayed. Selections of music from Saint-Saens' *The Carnival of the Animals*. Sketch of the Hindu elephant god Ganesha.

INTRODUCTION

Show the children the picture of Ganesha. Explain that this is one of the favourite gods in the Hindu religion. We are going to hear his story.

DISCUSS

Ask the children to speak about their favourite animals. Emphasize these points during the discussion:

- Animals give us a great deal of pleasure, especially through friendship, companionship, bravery, loyalty. What would the world be like without them?

- Some animals are exciting. What do you think about the lion, elephant and tiger. Because of their fierce nature and size, all of these fill humans with awe. Would you like to contribute ideas of your own about the feelings these and other animals inspire?

STORY

Long ago there lived a wicked and cruel Demon King. He had been promised by the god Shiva that no weapon, god or human would ever kill him, so he forced all the people in the world to bow down and worship him. They did so because they were afraid of him.

At last the people could not bear to worship the Demon King any longer. They went to Lord Shiva and begged him to set them free. In his garden, they saw a statue of two elephants' trunks twined together. The statue seemed to have a magical power.

Shiva told his wife to stand in front of the statue and to think very hard. The people watched and saw the Mother-Goddess change into two elephants who gave birth to a holy child which had four hands, and the head of an elephant. This was Ganesha, born to bring luck to the world.

Shiva commanded that Ganesha should spend all his life fighting evil. Ganesha hunted the Demon King. He broke off one of his own tusks and pierced his wicked enemy through the heart.

Since then, Hindu people have believed that the elephant god, Ganesha, is a sign of good luck, because he defeated evil. Ganesha is worshipped in many parts of western India.

The elephant is said to bring good luck in lots of places in the western world and is often a favourite animal of children. It is important that such animals should be protected by humans and helped to survive.

CONSIDER

Invite the children to consider one of these points:

- Wild animals such as elephants, lions and tigers are in danger of extinction because some humans hunt and kill them for their skins and tusks.

- Animals enrich the quality of life on Earth, just as the Hindu god Ganesha brought happiness to the people of India.

Many organisations, such as the World Wide Fund for Nature, work hard to help protect animals that are in danger. They do everything possible to make sure that animals like elephants continue to live on our planet.

HYMN

The children might sing this hymn, both as a prayer and as an aid to private reflection: *When God Made the Garden of Creation* (BBC hymn-book, *Come and Praise 1*).

MASTERS OF FLIGHT

Purpose To encourage thought on how birds are used as symbols and why.

Resources Any large, coloured posters of birds, particularly the eagle, dove or pigeon. It would be perfect to illustrate some of the points that are introduced if a child could arrange to bring a pigeon or budgie into school. A recording of ABBA's *Eagle song*, or the *Flight of the Condor*, or similar, which suggests birds in flight.

CONSIDER

Explain to the children that birds are important symbols for people throughout the world. Birds are often used as symbols of freedom, because of their ability to fly. Ask the children to close their eyes and imagine they are birds, free to fly in the wind wherever they like.

* The Jewish scriptures (the *Old Testament*, for Christians) say how Noah sent out a raven to see if it was safe to leave the Ark, during the Great Flood. When the raven did not return, Noah waited, and then sent out a dove. When the dove returned safely, carrying an olive branch in its beak, Noah knew that he could leave the Ark.

The dove has become a symbol of peace and the presence of God.

Some of you may be familiar with the pigeon, which belongs to the dove family. Many people find its soft 'cooing' call very soothing.

* The eagle is also a symbol for Christians, as well as one of the symbols of the Roman Empire. In Christian churches, eagle lecterns (or reading stands) are often used on which to rest the Bible or Prayer Book. The eagle is a strong bird, which can cover great distances in flight. It is a good symbol for the spread of religious teaching.

Hindus know the eagle as a sign of the god Varuna:

Longing for you in their heart, they saw you flying to the dome of the sky as an eagle, the golden-winged messenger.
(From the *Rig Veda*, Penguin, p.191)

Ask the children to point out the differences between the dove and the eagle, such as:

- The eagle is large and fierce; the dove seems soft and gentle.
- The eagle enjoys living in the wild; the dove lives near humans.

REFLECT

Ask the children if they can think of any way in which the modern aeroplane might be used as a religious symbol. Suggest some of these points as starters:

- Aeroplanes enable us to reach places very quickly and easily.

- They are very powerful.

- They can do what for thousands of years seemed impossible: they can fly.

- The largest, most expensive aeroplane is not nearly as efficient as a bird. Even the smallest bird flies much more naturally – it does not need an engine, a pilot, an airport.

- Aeroplanes bring help quickly to areas where there is famine or some other disaster. Air ambulances rescue people swiftly.

PRAY

Invite the children to think about this prayer:

> All things in Heaven and on Earth belong to Him;
> To Him be praise for evermore;
> He is the place of wisdom and He knows all things.
> He knows all that goes on in the Earth
> And all that comes out of it.
> (From *Sura* 34 of the *Qu'ran*.)

HYMN

Spirit of God (BBC hymn-book, *Come and Praise 1*).

GREEN

Purpose To teach the various meanings of the word 'green' and its use as a symbol of our concern for the environment and for conservation.

Resources Child or children dressed in green – costumes could be made from crêpe paper.

INTRODUCTION

Child or children dressed in green display their costumes. Which famous person in English history dressed in green? (Robin Hood) Why? (He wanted to hide among the trees and bushes of Sherwood Forest to avoid being captured by the Sheriff of Nottingham.) In this way, Robin Hood tried to make himself as close to nature as possible. You don't need to wear green now to be green but you do need to *think* green!

CONSIDER

What does the colour green remind you of?

- Go – at traffic lights?
- Grass, leaves, gardens, playing fields?
- Unleaded petrol?
- Conservation and environmental problems?

Has anyone heard of the 'green movement'? If you said that people were 'green' it used to mean that they were cowardly, envious, new to something, or even feeling sick! Now, to be 'green' also means that you believe in trying to:

- Save the natural world from being destroyed.
- Avoid wasting the resources of the world, such as forests, energy, plants and animals.
- Help to protect the countryside from pollution.
- Support the recycling movement: re-using glass and paper especially, instead of using precious natural resources to make more of these things.

REFLECT

How can we 'go green' without dressing up in green clothes?

- Keep the school field or yard and buildings tidy and litter free.
- Help animals and birds, because they are important to life.
- Ensure plants and trees are not damaged.
- Join a club or organisation which is trying to make the environment cleaner and safer.

HYMN

Invite the children to sing *All Things Bright and Beautiful* (BBC hymn-book, *Come and Praise 1*)

PRAY

The words of the hymn *All Things Bright and Beautiful* tell us much about the world of nature. Think about them:

All things bright and beautiful,
All creatures great and small,
All things wise and wonderful,
The Lord God made them all.

To 'go green' is to protect the beautiful things of our Earth.

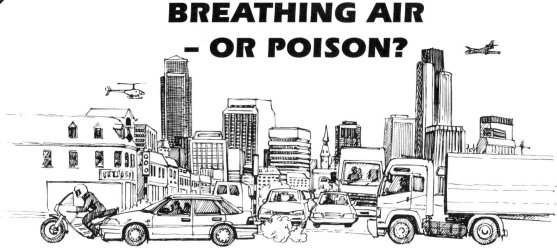

BREATHING AIR – OR POISON?

Purpose   To teach how our lifestyle endangers the Earth, particularly the air we breathe.

Resources   Two masks (to cover the mouth and nose).

INTRODUCTION

Let one child read:

And God saw everything that he had made, and behold, it was very good. (*Genesis 1, v. 31*)

Ask all the children to sit very still and to close their eyes. They should keep their shoulders still and not make a sound. Show them that they are breathing in and out to a pattern. Let them feel the air reaching their lungs and leaving them again.

- The air we have just breathed is quite clean BUT .....

CONSIDER

Two children enter who are wearing the masks. They face the others.

Tell the children that in many cities in Britain (and elsewhere) lots of people have begun to wear masks as they cycle or walk to work along streets where there is lots of traffic. One of the main reasons that the air is dirty and poisonous is because of the exhaust fumes from cars, buses and lorries. If the air was clean, no-one would have to wear masks.

The children take off their masks and read out:

- Fumes from a car's exhaust system are dirty and smelly. They can harm the air we breathe and the people who breathe it.

- Lead is sometimes added to petrol to make cars go better but lead is dangerous.

REFLECT

Let the children read out:

- Your family car does not have to be painted green to be green.

- Many cars can now run on unleaded petrol. They have a catalytic converter ('cat') in the engine which destroys poisonous fumes.

- A green car has a 'cat' and is a cleaner car.

- If all cars were green, people would not have to wear these masks (*the children show their masks again*).

- Find out if your car, or your friends' family cars, are green.

PRAY

These lines from Jewish scripture tell us that when God created the Earth it was good:

And God called the dry land Earth; and the gathering together of the waters called he seas; and God saw that it was good.
(*Genesis 1, v.10*)

Help us, God, to take care of the Earth,
doing everything we can to make sure it remains good.

HYMN

God Who Made The Earth (BBC hymn-book, *Come and Praise 1*).

ACID RAIN – BEWARE!

Purpose   To teach the children about the dangers of acid rain and its causes.

Resources   One glass of clean water. One glass of water containing a salt solution.

INTRODUCTION

Show the children the two glasses of water. Tell them that one is fresh but the other has had something added. Is it possible to tell which glass of water is clean just by looking? Invite a child to try tasting both glasses (explain that neither is dangerous).

CONSIDER

It is not always possible to understand everything just by using our eyes. Sometimes our eyes can make us believe something to be true when it might be false. It was necessary to taste the water to see which glass contained fresh water but we could only do this because we had been told that it was safe to do so.

Sometimes things that cause harm seem to be perfectly harmless. We can only learn by watching for results. This is what the Bible means when it says, 'By their fruits shall you know them'.

REFLECT

When the rain falls, it is very easy to think that the rain water is fresh simply because no-one has touched it. That is how it seems to be.

But when the rain falls, it has to pass through the Earth's atmosphere before it reaches the Earth itself. Our air, the atmosphere, is full of pollution – gases, fumes, dust and many chemicals that are produced by machines and other things we use, such as aerosol sprays. The falling rain collects these things and brings them down to Earth again.

We call the mixture 'acid rain'. It causes terrible damage.

Voice 1   Acid rain poisons the soil where farmers grow crops.
Voice 2   Acid rain pollutes the air and kills plants and trees.
Voice 3   Acid rain destroys the stonework of our buildings.

Who is to blame for acid rain? The answer is that we are – our way of life is to blame. This is a big problem that scientists and people who are worried about the Earth are trying to solve. The less pollution we cause, the less acid rain there will be.

When God made the world in the beginning, as Jewish and Christian scriptures tell us, the world was good. Can any of you suggest aspects of the world which are not so good today?

PRAY

These verses might be sung by the children as a hymn or read by them as a prayer for personal reflection:

> God of concrete, God of steel,
> God of piston and of wheel,
> God of pylon, God of steam,
> God of girder and of beam,
> God of atom, God of mine,
> All the world of power is thine.
>
> God whose glory fills the earth,
> Gave the universe its birth,
> Loosed the Christ with Easter's might,
> Saves the world from evil's blight,
> Claims mankind by grace divine,
> All the world of love is thine.
> (*100 Hymns for Today*, p.33)

21

HORROR PACKAGES

Purpose   To develop awareness of the dangers associated with fast-food packaging; also about making choices, understanding what we can do without.

Resources   A collection of fast-food packaging; for example, beefburger packets, polystyrene boxes, aerosol sprays, drink cans, plastic cartons or bottles.

INTRODUCTION

Invite a group of children to bring in and present a collection of different kinds of packaging and let them tell the others what each package once contained. At the end, the group of children chorus:

DO THE PACKAGES CONTAIN HORRORS FOR THE EARTH?

CONSIDER

Show the children the packages again. Say a few words about each:

- *Beefburger packets*   The box is probably made from polystyrene blown with chlorofluorocarbons (CFCs). This is the chemical largely responsible for destroying the Earth's protective ozone layer.

- *Plastic cartons*   Many plastic cartons are only used for a very short time but when they are dumped they might take hundreds of years to decompose. If they are burned in an incinerator, the fumes possibly give off harmful gases into the atmosphere which damage the ozone layer.

- *Aerosols*   Hair-spray, perfume – there are all kinds of different things in aerosol sprays. CFCs are often contained in them as well; they are used to push out whatever is in the spray. When they are released, the CFCs then do their share in destroying the ozone layer.

We are surrounded by packaging which is unnecessary and harmful.

STORY

There is a story from Jewish scriptures about a king called Solomon. He fell asleep and had a dream that God offered him a present. He had to choose one gift only.

Solomon thought very hard. He would like more gold to become richer. If he had more soldiers and weapons, he could capture more countries and make his own kingdom larger. If he had more slaves and servants, his own life would be easier. What should he ask for?

Then he understood something important. Gold, weapons and slaves would not make him a good king. Gold would make him greedy for more. Capturing other countries would cause suffering and unhappiness. He would become lazy if he had more slaves.

So Solomon asked God to make him wise, so that he might be a good king and able to see clearly which things in life were really important and which were unimportant and dangerous.

Like Solomon, we have the chance to make choices. We can decide what we really need and what we are better off without.

PRAY

Lord, help me to consider with care, when I buy things, whether the things I want are safe for our world and whether I really need them.

HYMN

Join With Us To Sing God's Praises (BBC hymn-book, *Come and Praise 1*).

WASTE NOT, WANT NOT

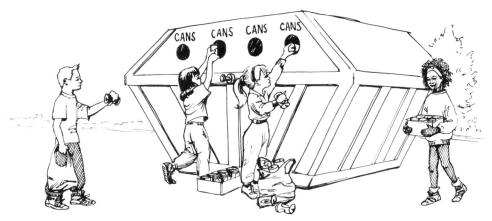

Purpose   To increase awareness of the need for careful use of resources, especially through recycling.

Resources   Samples of packing that might be recycled, such as newspaper, glass, drinks cans, clothes. Samples of recycled products, such as writing paper or kitchen rolls.

INTRODUCTION
Invite children to read out these proverbs:

- Waste not, want not.
- Waste makes want.
- Wilful waste makes woeful want.

It is more than 200 years since these proverbs, or wise sayings, were first written. They are very much in fashion today.

CONSIDER
Let the children hold up the samples of things that are thrown into bins every day:

- *Newspapers*   Paper is made from trees. Each person in Britain gets through six trees' worth of paper each year. Don't throw paper away with the rubbish. It can be used again, like these things made from recycled paper (see *Resources*). In many places, the people who collect your refuse also collect boxes of paper separately from other rubbish, or there are special collecting points nearby.

- *Glass bottles* If glass is not used again, it will lie in the ground forever and get broken and wasted. Have you seen a bottle bank? Put all the glass you have finished with in there (except milk bottles and others that can be refilled) and it will be taken away for recycling.

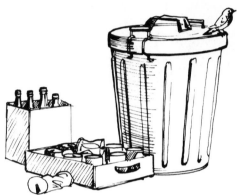

- *Cans* If cans are not re-used, what a waste of the metal that was used to make them! Put aluminium cans in a separate box from the rubbish (they are not magnetic and cannot be separated at the refuse plant).

- *Old clothes* Even these can be recycled. Oxfam and other charity shops will sell clothes second-hand. Clothes that are too old for anyone to use will be sent to the recycling centre, where they are sorted out and sent to mills.

REFLECT

We live in a very rich world. This is what the Book of Psalms tells us:

The heavens declare the glory of God;
and the firmament shows His handiwork.

(*Psalm 18*)

If we have a 'War on Waste', we can help to make sure that God's creation is used well and will continue to survive.

HYMN

Invite the children to think about the meaning of the lines and about our stewardship of the Earth.

Morning Has Broken (*New English Hymnal*).

UNDER ATTACK FROM LITTER

Purpose To discourage litter; to encourage the idea that litter is danger-ous, unsightly and makes our environment unpleasant and unhealthy.

Resources A collection of litter, in carrier bags. Outlines on card of leaf-less trees (probably two). Blue tac. Recording of ABBA's *Under Attack* (ABBA Gold cassette – this is optional). Gloves, to be worn by the children handling the litter.

INTRODUCTION

A group of children hold up their carrier bags. One child announces that some people have dropped things on the way to school or in the play-ground. What kinds of things have been lost?

In turn, the children show the others what they have found by holding up each object as it comes out of the bag.

CONSIDER

All the things displayed belong to the family of LITTER. What is the differ-ence between rubbish and litter? (Litter is rubbish that is carelessly dropped in the wrong place.)

Litter is very bad for our health and safety:

• It encourages flies, rats and mice, which spread disease.

• It makes us feel cross and depressed.

• It makes the town and the countryside look ugly.

• It can also be dangerous to domestic animals and wildlife.

Because we have so much litter lying around, you might say that Britain is 'under attack'. Something new and terrible is being planted in our land.

Play the ABBA recording of *Under Attack* while the children tack bits of litter onto the tree outlines.

REFLECT

Let the children read:

- Does anyone like the litter tree?
- It's very easy to stop litter trees from being planted.
- All we have to do is to keep this simple rule:

All together
Why not feed a litter bin?
Walk right up and drop it in!

PRAY

All that is in heaven and earth gives glory to God. He is a mighty king in glory. He has power over all things.
(*Qu'ran*)

Invite the children to think about this prayer:

Help me to keep the world tidy, Lord, by remembering not to throw away that little piece of paper in my pocket. Every little helps!

HYMN

Give Us Hope, Lord (BBC hymn-book, *Come and Praise 2*).

FAVOURITE FOOD?

Purpose   To encourage critical thought about the use of fast-foods and their effects on the wider environment.

Resources   An empty beefburger packet. Samples of soya beans, if available.

INTRODUCTION

Invite a group of children to read these lines to the others, who might like to guess the food described:

* I am dark red and get poured from a bottle, often onto chips. (*Tomato sauce*)
* I am golden brown, crispy and cut into rectangles. I usually get fried. (*Fish fingers*)
* I am round, brown and meaty. I am often served inside a bread bun or with chips. (*Beefburger*)
* I am round and golden brown; inside I have fish, sometimes even salmon. (*Fish cakes*)

CONSIDER

All these are examples of 'fast food', which means that they can all be prepared very quickly. Who has eaten any of these things? Who likes eating beefburgers or hamburgers? Why are these foods so popular? (They are cheap, easy to buy and to eat and they taste good.)

Many kinds of fast food are causing problems for the environment. Meat from cattle (beef) is used to make beefburgers but much of the land that is used for the cattle is not suitable for cattle farming. Large areas of rainforests have been cleared to make grazing land for the cattle but the grass does not grow well. More forests have to be cleared to provide more grass. The wildlife of the forests disappears.

Soya beans are now being fed to the cattle because they make them grow fatter more quickly and do not need so much land.

Remember   Huge areas of forest, and all the people, animals, birds and plants who lived there, are being destroyed for ever because so many people enjoy eating beefburgers!

REFLECT

What can we do to help the rainforests and all the living things that depend on them for their existence? If people did not buy burgers made from the meat of cattle who need to graze the land where the forests once grew, the making of beefburgers would gradually come to a stop. You can be sure that the burgers you eat come from land that used to be forest if the meat is from countries in central South America, such as Brazil or Argentina.

Let the children announce these lines:

- Ask the shopkeeper where the burger meat comes from.
- Find out what the cattle were fed on (grass or soya beans).
- Try to eat other kinds of food, such as vegetable burgers or bean burgers.

All together
THIS IS HOW YOU COULD HELP SAVE THE RAINFORESTS.

PRAY

God, help us to recognise the
beauty of the world and to do all
we can to preserve it.

HYMN

He Gave Me Eyes That I Could See (BBC hymn-book, *Come and Praise 1*).

TREASURES IN THE RAIN FOREST

Purpose   To teach about the links between aspects of the natural world and the importance of their preservation.

Resources   A globe. A collection of treasures inside a box; for example, brooches, beads, rings, small toys and figures.

INTRODUCTION

Tell the children that you have a treasure box. Invite them to come and pick a treasure from the box and show it to the others.

Why might some people call these things treasures?
What other kinds of treasure can the children think of?

Suggest that treasure might be anything that is very important to someone, especially if it cannot be replaced once it has gone.

CONSIDER

Point out on the globe the areas of the world where rainforests grow; for example, central America, central Africa, eastern Asia, the Philippines.

The rainforests might be thought of as a kind of treasure. They contain many tribes of people and varieties of wildlife that would disappear forever if the forests are destroyed. We will not be able to replace the life that disappears.

- Thousands of rainforest plants, which cannot be grown anywhere else, provide many of the medicines that can be seen in chemist's shops; for example, the Rosy Periwinkle, which grows in the Amazon rainforest, is used in the treatment of leukaemia in children.

- Animals, insects and birds depend for their food and survival upon the trees and plants in rainforests. The food chain in the forests provides for the needs of all the creatures that live there, including the people.

REFLECT

Let the children present these facts about rainforests themselves:

- As rainforests are cut down, the plants and animals which live there die.
- Each forest plays a part in the balance of nature; that is, the survival of plants, animals and trees.
- While species of plants are disappearing, we may be losing forever the cures for many diseases.

YOU can help save the rainforest by encouraging your family NOT to buy things made from tropical wood, such as mahogany or teak. If you do buy these woods, loggers will cut down even more trees.

YOU can help by telling people how the plants which grow in rainforests are so important in the making of medicines.

YOU can help by talking about the importance of rainforests to your family and friends.

HYMN

For The Beauty Of The Earth (BBC hymn-book, *Come and Praise 1*).

PRAY

Invite the children to think about this and to respond in their own way:

Thank you, God, for this world that you have planned.
Help us to follow the plan of creation in our own lives. Amen.

AWE AND WONDER

THE BIG BANG
OF CREATION

Purpose   To introduce the idea of God being a controlling, living but mysterious power working within and through the universe.

Resources   A suitable piece of listening music is *The Heavens are Telling*, from Haydn's *Creation* oratorio.

INTRODUCTION

Invite the children to read these lines from the Jewish and Christian scriptures which give some idea of how human beings try to understand the idea of God creating the world:

In the beginning God created the heaven and the earth. And the earth was without form, and void: and darkness was upon the face of the waters.

(Jewish and Christian scriptures, *Genesis 1, vv.1-2*)

CONSIDER

The words that you have just heard come from a poem that was written thousands of years ago, to praise God who created the Earth. The energy in life that is concerned with good things and opposed to bad things, Christians call God, Hindus call Brahman, Muslims call Allah, Jews call YHWH.

There was neither non-existence nor existence then; there was neither the realm of space nor the sky which is beyond. What stirred? Where?
(Hindu scriptures, the *Rig Veda*, the Creation hymn)

To God belongs everything in the heavens and in the earth.
(Islamic scriptures, the *Qu'ran 3 v.123*)

What do these readings say about Creation? They say that there was only one God at the beginning and that he made the whole Universe from nothing.

REFLECT

The world religions all say that Creation is a mystery. This is clear in the Hindu writing. But they all say that a God, a force of energy, is the cause of Creation. Science tries to tell us how the laws of the Universe work but science does not tell us what is the meaning or purpose of life.

Invite the children to listen to a short extract from *The Heavens Are Telling* .

PRAY

Invite the children to listen to this prayer about the power and might of God and to consider whether they agree with it:

> Even the sky and the earth bow low before him,
> and the mountains are terrified of his hot breath;
> he who is known as the 'drinker of power', with the
> thunderbolt in his hand, with the thunderbolt in
> his palm, he, my people, is God.
> (Paraphrase of Hindu scripture, the *Rig Veda,*
> *Indra*)

HYMN

Glory Be To Thee, My God, This Night (Hymns Ancient and Modern, vv. 1,4,6).

FORCE OF FIRE

Purpose   To teach the use of fire as a religious symbol of God's presence.

Resources   Red crêpe paper, sticks and a torch, to make a model fire; or a couple of candles.

INTRODUCTION

Invite the children to look at the imitation fire or candles. As they observe, ask the children to read:

• The fire which lights us from a distance will burn us when near.

• No smoke without fire.

• Out of the frying pan into the fire.

• Violent fires soon burn out.

CONSIDER

These are all proverbs, or wise sayings. Although they all mention fire, none of them are really about fire. Can anyone suggest ideas as to what the proverbs mean?

• Something when it is far off might be helpful but when it is too close it might be harmful.

• If you see a clue, you can be sure that something's happened.

• Getting out of one mess into another, even worse.

• Outbreaks of temper, or bad storms, are soon over.

REFLECT

Fire has been used as a symbol from the very earliest times. Why should that be? It gives light and warmth; it is useful; it is exciting and dangerous; it has movement, a life of its own.

There are many stories in religion that use fire as a symbol of God, or his power. Here is one of them:

The Jewish scriptures (the Christian *Old Testament*) tell of the time when Moses was in the desert looking after his father-in-law's flocks of sheep and goats. Moses came to a mountain and saw a flame in the middle of a bush. He saw that the bush appeared to burn and yet it was not damaged.

Moses realised that the flame, in some mysterious way, was a symbol of God. He knew that he was close to God as he looked at the burning bush.

PRAY

Invite the children to think about these lines:

> Like quivering tongues of light and flame,
> Upon each one the Spirit came:
> Tongues that the earth might hear their call,
> And fire, that love might burn in all.
> (From *Rejoice, The Year Upon Its Way*, New English Hymnal)

HYMN

Flickering Candles In The Night (BBC hymn-book, *Come and Praise 2*).

THE HEAVENS ARE TELLING

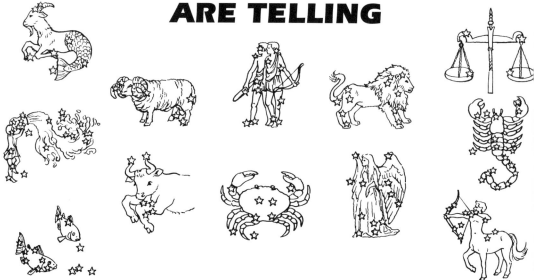

Purpose   To introduce ideas about God that are linked with human fascination with outer space.

Resources   A recording of extracts from Gustav Holst's *The Planets*; for example, *Jupiter, Bringer of Jollity*.

INTRODUCTION

What are planets? They are heavenly bodies that move around the Sun. The Earth is one of the nine planets that have been discovered so far within our own solar (or sun) system.

CONSIDER

Here are some ideas that people long ago had about outer space:

- The planets made beautiful music as they moved around. People called this 'the music of the spheres'.

- It was believed that you could read your fortune from looking at your constellation, or group of stars. Ask the children if they read their stars in the newspaper. Do they believe in astrology? Do they know their birth-sign? The names were given to the constellations by the Ancient Greeks.

- When Yuri Gagarin, the first human astronaut, returned from space, he said that he was surprised that he did not see God during his journey through the Universe! What do you think he meant?

- Religious people believe that God made the Universe and continues to keep it in motion. Is there any good reason for us to expect to find God in the Universe? Can you see:

- The engineer inside a radio that he or she made?
- The clockmaker inside a clock that he or she made?
- The shoemaker inside a pair of shoes that he or she made?
- A cook inside the meal that he or she prepared?

If you cannot see them, why should people expect to find God inside the Universe which many believe he made?

Invite the children to listen to an extract from *The Planets*. Afterwards, you might tell the children what the music is, and how the composer, Gustav Holst, took his idea for the melody from thinking about the planets themselves.

REFLECT

Some astronomers, or people who study the objects in outer space, tell us that the Universe has no end. It stretches on forever.

Close your eyes and try to imagine space stretching on and on and on, never coming to an end. What happens to your mind when you try to imagine this? Does your mind simply shut off?

PRAY

Here are a few lines from scriptures that tell us something about people's ideas of God:

Praise you the Lord.
Praise you the Lord from the heavens;
praise him in the heights.
Praise you him, sun and moon,
praise him, all you stars of light.
Praise you, you heavens of heavens,
and you waters that be above the heavens.
(*Psalm 148*, Jewish scripture, Christian *Old Testament*)

HYMN

Every Star Shall Sing a Carol (*100 Hymns for Today*, Clowes 1972).

HAVE YOU SEEN MONSTERS?

Purpose   To introduce the idea of good and evil in conflict and the hope that good will prove to be the stronger.

Resources   Pictures of dinosaurs or other monsters. Recording of *In the Hall of the Mountain King* by Grieg (or any music suggesting the movement of heavy animals).

INTRODUCTION

We hear of many kinds of monsters. Invite the children to name a few. One thing that monsters have in common is that they are frightening. Suggest that the children close their eyes and listen to the music of Grieg.

Did anyone hear anything like the monsters' footsteps in the music? Many people do hear them.

STORY

A prince called Petros was sailing home when his ship was caught in a storm and wrecked on an unknown island. Petros managed to clamber ashore and fell exhausted on the beach. When he woke, he found himself surrounded by a crowd of anxious people.

They told him about their troubles. A terrible monster, called the Shoba, lived in a den nearby, deep in the forest, and each morning stalked through the town, searching for someone to eat for breakfast. Many had tried to kill the monster but it was too evil to be destroyed.

Petros said to the people, 'I'm a stranger and yet you didn't harm me when I lay defenceless on the beach. In thanks for that, I shall destroy this monster for you.'

He went with the townsfolk to their market place, where they gave him food and where he waited for the monster, armed only with a little dagger. The Shoba came with a terrible roar and the townsfolk fled with screams of terror.

'Shoba,' shouted Petros, as the beast came lumbering up the street, 'I have no wish to harm you. Why do you prey on the people of this town, killing and devouring them?'

This was the first time that anyone had ever spoken kindly to the monster. It dropped its green, scaly head in astonishment and looked at Petros. 'If you don't want to fight me, why are you holding that dagger?' it asked.

Petros replied, 'I was about to give you half the meat I had this morning.' So he cut the steak the people had given him and offered half to the huge beast.

It shook its head. 'No,' said the Shoba. 'You are too kind. If you had meant to harm me, I would have killed you but I cannot defeat kindness. I shall leave this island in peace now.'

Petros watched joyfully as the monster made its way down to the shore. It swam into the ocean and was never seen again.

REFLECT

Jesus once said that if anyone hit you – for example, on your cheek – you should turn the other cheek for them to hit as well. In that way, you would make them feel a fool and they would leave you alone.

He taught that good is stronger than evil and that evil will always make things worse.

PRAY

The words of this hymn might be used as a prayer:

When A Knight Won His Spurs (BBC hymn-book, *Come and Praise 1*) or *Who Would True Valour See.*

HYMN

Make Me A Channel Of Your Peace (*Worship Songs, Hymns Ancient and Modern*).

CRYSTALS OF ICE AND SNOW

Purpose   To encourage children to think about cold winter weather as exciting – a time which for many is a challenge; to think of winter as a symbol of life itself.

Resources   An extract recording from Vivaldi's *Four Seasons: Winter*. T-shirts, gloves, scarves, hats, shorts, boots, slippers, sweaters (a mixture of clothes for cold and warm days).

INTRODUCTION

Ask the children to share their ideas about what the word 'winter' makes them think; for example, icicles, snow, Christmas, frost, slides.

CONSIDER

Produce samples of clothing from a bag. Invite the youngest children to comment on which clothes they would wear for playing out in the snow.

POEM

Invite children to read their own poems. Here is one:

> Winter, winter, lovely winter,
> Children playing in the snow,
> Sledging, sliding all about.
> Here comes a blizzard, it all goes quiet.
> Then the snow man tucks himself in bed.
> Winter is over.

(Mark Ridley, Dipton Collierley Primary School, Co. Durham)

PRAY

The cold weather certainly makes life more difficult but it also makes us keep on the move. The following Christian prayer thanks God for keeping us lively, for 'stirring us up'.

Stir up, we ask you, O Lord, the lives of your people, that they may enjoy all the good things which were created, and feel happy.
(based on the Collect of the 25th Sunday after Trinity, the *Book of Common Prayer*)

> Thank you for glittering snow and slippery slides,
> Ice and snowballs, sledges and rides.
> For all the fun that winter brings,
> We give you thanks for all these things.

MUSIC

Play the extract from Vivaldi's *Four Seasons: Winter*, or a well-known song such as *Jingle Bells*.

HYMN

Lay My White Cloak (BBC hymn-book, *Come and Praise 2*).

THE WORLD - OUR SYMBOL

THE LOTUS FLOWER

Purpose   To teach the children about the Hindu and Buddhist symbol of the Lotus Flower and what it can mean to all of us.

Resources   Picture of a lotus flower. Picture of a Hindu lamp – the lotus flower shape has been used for the holder, in which a candle has been placed. Beethoven's *Pastoral Symphony*.

INTRODUCTION

Explain to the children that flowers are important to many different religious faiths. The lotus flower is a symbol for the Hindu faith and for followers of the Buddha, a great spiritual leader.

STORY

This story is about a very deep lake.The bottom of the lake is filled with thick, black mud. There are many lakes like this in India and what happens in this story happens over and over again every year.

Once upon a time, a flower seed fell into the lake. It sank down, down, down, through the water, until it reached the mud at the bottom.

After some time the seed put out roots – tiny little roots like the finest hairs. The plant was starting to grow. When it felt its roots were firm, it began to grow a stalk, which became longer and longer, feeling its way up through the waters of the lake, up and up, leaving the thick, black mud behind.

The stalk grew until at last it pushed through the surface waters of the lake. A bud had formed on the end of the stalk and it began to open as the warm sun of India shone on it. There soon appeared a beautiful white flower, so lovely that all the passing people stopped to marvel at its shape and size and colour.

'To think that such a lovely flower could have grown out of such a deep and muddy lake!' someone said.

'That's the lotus flower,' said someone else. 'It's trying to tell us something.'

'I know what it's saying,' said a child. 'Even when everything's against us – no money, a broken down house, or even worse – we can do great things in our lives!'

'That's right,' said the first person. 'We could learn a lesson from that flower. We should never give up.'

Buddhists sit in the 'lotus position' when they meditate. Their hope is that they will have the faith and success of the lotus flower, that they will grow out of the 'mud' of their own lives.

REFLECT
Invite the children to sit quite still and with their eyes closed to think about the story they have just heard. Comments that some children might like to offer would be valuable.

HYMN
Lord Of All Hopefulness (BBC hymn-book, *Come and Praise 1*).

PRAY

Help my mind rise above ugliness and cruelty,
Above worries and the things that upset me
During the day – spelling tests and bullies,
Losing my belongings or quarrelling wth friends.

These are the things which prevent me enjoying life.
Help me to recognise things of real importance.

MUSIC
Let the children listen to some music, such as Beethoven's *Pastoral Symphony*, to conclude the Worship.

SEA SECRETS

Purpose   To stimulate awareness of the mystery of the sea and its associated symbolism.

Resources   Recording of Mendelssohn's *Fingal's Cave* Overture (or any music reminiscent of the sea). A display of sea-shells, seaweed, rocks. Pictures of sea-creatures drawn or painted by children. Prints of seascapes, such as *The Steam Ship* by Turner.

INTRODUCTION

Let the children listen to *Fingal's Cave* as they arrive in the assembly hall. Invite them to to offer their own ideas about the music. Did they, for example, find it exciting, frightening, sad or happy?

Tell them that the music was composed by Felix Mendelssohn after listening to the sea echoing through the caves on the island of Staffa on the western coast of Scotland nearly 200 years ago.

Let the children listen to a short extract from the music again. Can they hear the sea in the melody?

CONSIDER

Let some children tell the others about items in the display. What effect does the sea have upon stones, glass or weed? (It makes them smooth.) If there is a large shell in the collection, ask children to volunteer to put it to their ear so they can listen to the 'sound of the sea'.

Invite children to read out these statements about the sea:

• Two-thirds of the Earth's surface is covered by sea.

• There are parts of the sea-bed that cannot be reached by humans because of the depth of the water.

• There are mountains under the sea that are higher than the tallest mountain on dry land (Mt Everest).

- The sea can be beautiful or ugly, frightening or exciting; it can be a means of transport or a barrier to travel.

- The sea is never still.

REFLECT

Our lives are like the sea in some ways, full of excitement, danger and opportunities for doing new things. Jesus told his disciples that they were going to be like fishermen when they taught people about God, but they would not be trying to catch fish in the 'sea of life', they would be trying to win people for God.

HYMN

The words of this hymn could be used as a prayer instead:

And I Listen (BBC hymn-book, *Come and Praise 1*).

PRAY

Thank you, God, for such an exciting world, and especially for the sea and the fishermen who risk their lives to bring us food; help us to remember them and all the people who help us in any way.

WE LOOK – AND SEE!

Purpose To consider that the world may be seen in many different ways and that we will discover new things about life each day, just as we may discover new things about God each day.

Resources Some diagrams of 'perspective pictures', drawn on large sheets of card.

INTRODUCTION

Have any of the children ever seen a giant? We all see giants every day but we don't necessarily view them as giants. What about ourselves? Could we be giants? Encourage the children to think about small animals to which humans would definitely appear gigantic and probably rather frightening.

STORY

The Blind Men and the Elephant

This is a traditional Hindu story. A number of blind men all felt different parts of an elephant, trying to work out what it was like. This is what happened:

- The first man felt its leg and thought it was like a tree trunk.

- The second felt its trunk and said it was like a snake.

- The third felt its tusks and said it was like a spear.

- The fourth felt its tail and said it was like a rope.

- The fifth felt its ear and said it was like a leaf.

- The sixth felt its side and said it was like a wall.

Were any of the men right or wrong?

They were all right, of course, but only right in part. What we see is usually only part of the whole thing.

CONSIDER

Show the children the perspective pictures. Give them a few moments for reflection and ask them what they can see in the pictures. Is anybody wrong? Who is to say, for example, that the candlestick picture is not a picture of two faces?

We all tend to see things in different ways. Sometimes we might be wrong but sometimes there can be more than one correct answer. What we see depends on how we look at things.

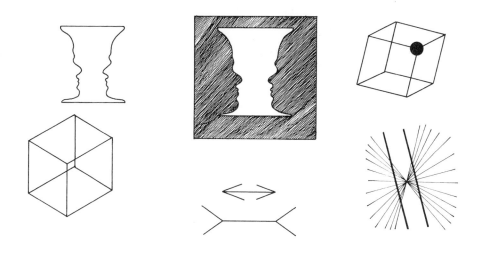

REFLECT

This is how some of the great world religions help us to understand God:

> From him the universe comes, he who teaches
> Each living creature to be perfect,
> According to its own kind. He is
> The Lord of Love who reigns over all life.
> (Hindu scripture, *The Upanishads*, Penguin p.228)

> A thousand years to you, God, are just like
> yesterday when they are over.
> (From *Psalm 90*, Jewish scripture)

There are many different ways of thinking about God – each may be right and all are needed. They are like signposts pointing toward the truth.

HYMN

He's Got The Whole World In His Hands (BBC hymn-book, *Come and Praise 1*).

HUNTERS AND SEARCHERS

Purpose To tell the story of the Good Shepherd, a parable showing how God cares for his people as a good shepherd cares for his sheep.

INTRODUCTION

Explain to the children that the word 'hunt' has more than one possible meaning. Ask the children to give examples of what the word 'hunt' means to them. This should enable their values to be expressed.

Invite two or three children to begin hunting for something which you have hidden in the hall earlier. When it has been found, show how delighted you are to have the article back.

CONSIDER

Have any of the children hunted? (If they answer 'no', ask if anyone has ever lost anything and searched for it. If they have, then they have been a hunter.) Everybody will hunt for something they have lost if they think it is important.

STORY

Jesus told a few stories about hunting. Here is one:

The Lost Sheep (*Matthew 18, vv.10-12*)

> A shepherd once had a hundred sheep. He counted them before he took them out onto the hills. At sunset he returned with them to the farm and counted them again. One day, to his horror, he found there were only ninety-nine. He shut

48

them safely in a pen and made his way back to the hillside to look for the one that was lost. After a long search, he found the sheep trapped in a thorn bush.

Full of joy, he set it free and carried it carefully on his shoulders back to the farm to rejoin the rest of the flock.

Jesus taught that God is like the shepherd in some ways. He is concerned about his people. If someone begins to lead a life which is bad, such as stealing, being spiteful, or bullying, God will try to rescue them and bring them back to a good way of living. If he succeeds, God will be just as joyful as the shepherd who found his lost sheep.

In that way, God may be thought of as a hunter – he hunts for people who need help.

PRAY OR HYMN

Invite a child to read this version of *The Lord Is My Shepherd*, or let the children sing it together:

The Lord is my shepherd,
I shall not want.
He makes me lie down in green pastures,
He leads me beside peaceful waters.
He feeds my soul:
He leads me on safe paths for his own sake.
Although I walk in fear of death
I shall not be afraid
Because God is with me
And I shall be comforted.

LIGHT THROUGH DARKNESS

Purpose To introduce the religious symbols of light and darkness and to explore their use.

Resources A lit candle.

HYMN

Perhaps you could start the assembly with a hymn to set the mood.
Be Thou My Vision (*New English Hymnal*).

INTRODUCTION

Remind the children how the sun lights up the Earth each morning. Ask them to watch the candle burning for a few moments and to think what light means to them.

CONSIDER

Everyone has been afraid of darkness at some time in their life. Here are some things that nine-year-old children have written about light and darkness and what it meant to them (to be read by the children):

• When I lie in bed in the dark I feel terrified of monsters. When I switch on my light I feel fine again.

• I was in darkness when I lost my grandma in the shop. When I saw her coming round the counter I was in light again.

• Once, I got home before my mother. I was in darkness because I thought she had been knocked down or something like that. I was very, very worried but, when I saw her coming, I came into light.

• A lighthouse shines out in the darkness and guides ships through the rocks to safety. The lighthouse gives light in a dangerous, dark sea.

REFLECT

Jesus is sometimes called 'the Light of the World'. Christians believe that Jesus is rather like the lighthouse – his 'light' is what he taught and the example he gave to people.

Muslims, in their Holy Book, the *Qu'ran*, read these lines:

> God is the light of the heavens and of the earth.
> His light is like a shelf that holds a lamp
> within a crystal of star-like light.
> (*Qu'ran 24 v.35, Light*)

PRAY

Here is a Hindu prayer to think about:

Lead us from the darkness to the light,
Lead us from lies to the truth.
Lead us from death to everlasting life.

HYMN

From The Darkness Came Light (BBC hymn-book, *Come and Praise 1*).

ROCK OF STRENGTH

Purpose   To teach how rock is an important symbol of God.

Resources   A few rock specimens.

INTRODUCTION

Show the children the rocks. Rocks are often used in writings about God or religion and faith. An old Christian hymn begins:

> Rock of ages, cleft for me,
> Let me hide myself in thee.

'Cleft' means 'cut open'. Perhaps the writer was thinking about a cave, somewhere secret, where anyone hiding would feel safe. A really big rock, that you could hang on to for support, might also make you feel safe.

CONSIDER

Rocks are important in our lives and are used for many things. Can anyone suggest ways in which we use rocks (building, roads, gravestones).

We use rocks because they are strong. They last a long time. Buildings have to be strong to stand against wind, rain and sometimes storm. Rocks, or stones, are good building materials.

STORY

Retell the story of *The Three Little Pigs*. The Ladybird Book version is very popular.

REFLECT

Jesus told a story about two men who built themselves houses. The first man built his house on sand. It did not have good foundations because sand moves. When a storm came, with floods, the house fell down, crash! The second man built his house on rock. He dug deep foundations and when the storm came the house stood firmly.

Jesus taught his followers that people who try hard to do their best to follow God's way are like the man who built his house on rock. They are like a rock themselves. They are people you know you can trust.

Jesus said that his friend and disciple, Peter, was a rock. What sort of person was Peter, do you think?

PRAY

Invite the children to listen to this prayer from the *Qu'ran*:

I seek safety with the Lord of people,
The King of people, the Judge of people,
From the evil whisperings
In the hearts of people.
(From the *Qu'ran*, Sura 114)

HYMN

Invite the children to join in singing, or follow the words of:

The Lord Of The Dance (BBC hymn-book, *Come and Praise 1*).

WATER OF LIFE

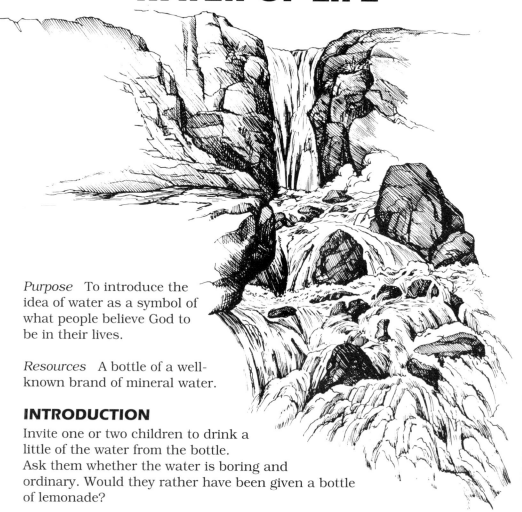

Purpose To introduce the idea of water as a symbol of what people believe God to be in their lives.

Resources A bottle of a well-known brand of mineral water.

INTRODUCTION

Invite one or two children to drink a little of the water from the bottle.
Ask them whether the water is boring and ordinary. Would they rather have been given a bottle of lemonade?

Other drinks may be more exciting but we must have water to survive. Water is used in the making of all the drinks that we enjoy.

CONSIDER

It is impossible for life to continue without water. Ask the children what we need it for (drinking, washing, cooking, making plants grow, travelling on, enjoyment). Without water, the land would become desert, a bleak place with no plants, few animals and birds, and most uncomfortable for people unless they have the correct equipment. Even our bodies are made up mostly of water.

Religious people find water a good symbol of what they believe God to be in their lives, whether God is called Allah, Brahman or YHWH. Has anyone any idea of how God can be said to be like water?

(Perhaps religious people feel that God is essential for a reasonably happy life. Without God, life would become like a desert. What does that mean?)

STORY

Jacob is one of the heroes of Judaism. Jewish scriptures tell us that, as a young man, he was very unhappy because of trouble in his family. One warm afternoon, Jacob sat down in the shade to rest near a well, when a girl, a cousin whom he had never met before, came to get water for her sheep and lambs. Her name was Rachel.

As Jacob helped her, he thought how beautiful she was and he began to feel much happier. In much the same way that he drew water from the well, so a new kind of 'water of life' surged up inside him.

Later, Jacob married Rachel and they had many children. One of them was called Joseph.

(From *Genesis 29, vv. 1-11*)

HYMN

Invite the children to join in the following hymn or to follow the words. What might they mean?

Jesus Gives Us The Water Of Life (BBC hymn-book, *Come and Praise 1*).

PRAY

God, thank you for the gift of life-giving water.

THE WORLD AROUND US

STREETS AND PEOPLE

Purpose   To help the children to understand that people are the most important thing wherever anyone lives.

Resources   A display of paintings by some of the children of the streets where they live.

INTRODUCTION
Invite some of the children to tell the others the names of the streets where they live and to show them their paintings.

CONSIDER
Did anyone hear the name of their own street mentioned or did they recognise any of the streets from the paintings?

Ask the childen to indicate if any of these things can be found in their street:

Houses	Lamp-posts
Church	Pavements
School	Cars
Shops	Telephone box
Pub	Litter bin

What has been missed from the list so far? PEOPLE!

REFLECT

People are the most important things in a street. Why is this? Because the street has been made by people, for people, and it is people who make it what it is today – tidy, ugly, dirty, clean, pleasant, boring, exciting, colourful.

Ask the children what might be put in the street to make it more –

- Cheerful (perhaps flowers, carefully painted doors)

- Interesting (perhaps trees, unusual gardens)

Is there anything in the street they would like to see taken away?

- Litter?

- Gardens filled with rubbish?

- Broken-down fences?

- Graffiti?

Everybody gives something to the street where they live. The street can be thought of as a painting that is being painted by many people.

PRAY

Next time I walk up my street, help me to remember the many people who live there and to think especially of the the old or the sick when I am playing and enjoying myself, so that I will not disturb them.

HYMN

The Family Of Man (BBC hymn-book, *Come and Praise 1*).

HUMANS AND FLOWERS

Purpose   To show that flowers have practical uses for people.

Resources   Pictures or examples of sunflowers, comfrey, dandelion, foxglove. A print of Van Gogh's *Sunflowers*. A margarine tub and a cooking-oil container illustrated with sunflowers. Specimens of dandelion clocks – depending on the time of year!

INTRODUCTION

Did you know that flowers help to save people's lives every day?

CONSIDER

Foxglove   It grows in woods and forests. It has pretty pink bells, although sometimes these may be white. In some districts it is called 'Fairy Bells'. This flower is deadly poisonous (so are many other wild flowers) and yet it also provides a drug called digitalis, which is used to help people with heart trouble, to make their hearts stronger.

Comfrey   A wild flowering plant, common throughout the British Isles. It is white, blue or purple. In the Middle Ages, its roots were ground to powder and mixed with water to make a sludge to pack around broken bones to help them set. For this reason, comfrey is sometimes called 'knitbone' or 'boneset'. In the Fifteenth Century the ground-up roots, mixed with ale, were drunk to help back pain. Today the root is mixed with sugar and liquorice to make a cough medicine.

Dandelion This common British plant gets its name from the shape of its leaves – in French, *dent-de-lion* (lion's tooth). In past times, it was used to treat diseases like jaundice and consumption. Its leaves are full of Vitamin A and C. When young, the leaves can be used in salads. A delicious wine can be made from the flowers. Country people used to grate its roots to obtain a powder which they used instead of coffee. If dandelion clocks are available, invite the children to 'to tell the time' by blowing away the seed-head. Mention that plants spread their seeds by many different methods.

Sunflowers A popular garden plant with a large face that follows the sun round. It provides us with sunflower oil to use for cooking and for making margarine. Ask the children if they have seen either of these being used at home. It is grown as a crop by farmers. A large field of sunflowers is a beautiful sight in late summer.

STORY

An old Greek story relates that the sunflower was once a young girl who fell in love with Apollo, the god who drove the sun across the sky each morning. The maiden used to brush out her golden hair and smile at Apollo, hoping he would see her. But he failed to notice her, no matter how long she watched the sun. Eventually her feet became fixed to the earth and she changed into a flower with a beautiful golden head that watches the sun each day, just as the girl had done.

HYMN

O Lord, All The Earth (BBC hymn-book, *Come and Praise 1*).

PRAY

God, thank you for the gift of flowers and all other good things which come from them.

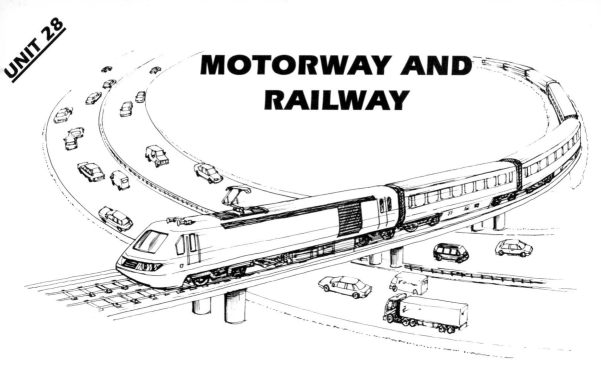

MOTORWAY AND RAILWAY

Purpose   To draw attention to the need to protect wild flowers and ways in which they seed in new areas as old habitats are destroyed.

Resources   Pictures of wild flowers, perhaps as shown on birthday or greetings cards, which will be familiar to the children.

INTRODUCTION

Ask the children if anyone has seen wildflowers growing or has ever picked one. Wild flowers bring great pleasure to many people. Some of those which grow in Britain do not grow in any other countries. They need to be protected because many are disappearing quickly from some parts of Britain.

CONSIDER

The use of chemicals has killed many meadow flowers, such as the primrose and the bluebell. The primrose, with its lovely splash of pale yellow, has nearly disappeared from the countryside because people have dug up plants to put them in their own gardens.

Have you ever seen bluebells growing? The bluebell is really a wild hyacinth. You may have seen hyacinths in pots indoors in the winter. In woods, in the spring, a carpet of wild bluebells can be a wonderful sight. It would be impossible to count them all. But the bluebell is in danger because people have pulled up huge numbers of their bulbs to replant at home.

Even so, a miracle is happening in Britain. After years of being attacked, wildflowers are starting to grow in new places that are safe from chemicals used by farmers and gardeners and that are far away from the footpaths trodden by visitors.

60

REFLECT

Ask the children where they think these safe places might be.

Have any of the children seen wild flowers growing on the banks of motorways or railway lines. Remind the children of the dangers to humans near these places. The flowers are safe but we would not be.

During the past thirty years, motorways have been built to connect our cities. Walkers are not allowed on the motorways. But the grass borders have become homes for the wildflowers that used to live in woods and hegerows. They are safe from humans and our careless ways.

Let the children have a moment for quiet reflection.

HYMN

Lord Of The Harvest (BBC hymn-book, *Come and Praise 1*).

PRAY

Invite the children to read alternate lines:

Thank you for the beauty of the countryside, especially for:

bluebells growing deeply in woods,
primroses in the shelter of hedges,
the pleasure that all wildflowers bring
and our growing understanding
of their needs.

REFERENCES AND USEFUL ADDRESSES

Please send a large stamped addressed envelope if you write to charities.

REFERENCES FOR UNITS 1-5 WILD LIFE

Delin, H. & Svensson, L. (1988) *The Photographic Guide to the Birds of Britain & Europe*, The Book People, ISBN 0-600-55808-8

Fitter, R., Fitter, A. & Blamely, M. (1974) *The Wildflowers of Britain and Europe*, Collins, ISBN 0-00-211278-7

Horowitz, A. (1985) *The Kingfisher Book of Myths and Legends*, Kingfisher Books, ISBN 0-86272-786-3

Jaroslav, S.D. & Solovjev, J. (1982) *Spotting Birds – A Pocket Guide to Bird Watching*, Hamlyn, ISBN 0-600-03614-6

Keble Martin, W. (1972) *The Concise British Flora in Colour*, Sphere Books

Palmer, J. (1986) *Time for Trees*, Dryad Press, ISBN 08521-9646-6

Reader's Digest Association (ed) (1981) *Field Guide to the Wild Flowers of Britain*, Reader's Digest Association, ISBN 0-276-00217-2

Vedel, H. & Lange, J. (1968) *Trees and Bushes in Wood and Hedgerow*, Methuen, ISBN 416-61780-8

Vevers, G. (1990) *The Natural World*, Colour Library Books

USEFUL ADDRESSES

The Wild Flower Society
68 Outwoods Road
Loughborough
Leics LE11 3LY

The Royal Society for Nature Conservation
The Green
Nettleham
Lincoln LN2 2NR

The Royal Society for the Protection of Birds
Freepost
Sandy
Beds SG19 2BR

REFERENCES FOR UNITS 6-13 OUR ENVIRONMENT

(Books providing information for teachers)

Anderson, W. (1990) *The Green Man: The Archetype of our Oneness with the Earth*, Harper Collins, ISBN 0-06-250075-9

Ashton, E. (1992) 'The Green Man and Religious Education', *RE Today*, Spring 1993

Bronze, L., Heathcote, N. & Brown, P. (1990) *The Blue Peter Green Book*, BBC Books, ISBN 0-563-20886-4

Morrison, M. (1993) *The Amazon Rainforest*, Wayland, ISBN 0-7502-0484-2

Palmer, J. (1986) *Time for Trees*, Dryad, ISBN 0-8521-9646-6

Thomas, J. (1990) *Population and Food*, Gloucester Press, ISBN 0-7496-0077-2

USEFUL ADDRESSES

Friends of the Earth
26/28 Underwood Street
Islington
London N1 7JQ

Greenpeace
Canonbury Villas
Islington
London N1 2PN

HBMC (English Heritage)
Saville Row
London W1X 1AB

People's Trust for Endangered Species
Hamble House
Meadowrow
Godalming
Surrey GU7 3JX

World Wide Fund for Nature
Panda House
Weyside Park
Godalming
Surrey GU7 1XR

A work scheme called 'Creation' (for 9-11 year-olds; send 50p SAE + £1) is available from:

Dr B.G. Watson
Wyke House
Croft Bank
West Malvern
Worcs WR14 4BP

REFERENCES FOR UNITS 14-18 AWE AND WONDER

(Sources of ideas for concept development)

Morin, D. (1990) *How to Understand God*, SCM, ISBN 0-334-02451

Poole, M. (1990) *Science and Belief*, Lion, ISBN 0-7324-0243-3

Nicholson, I. et al. (1989) *The Nature of the Universe*, Equinox, Ref. CN 2768

REFERENCES FOR UNITS 19-28 THE WORLD – OUR SYMBOL and THE WORLD AROUND US

Ashton, E. (1993) 'Rock of Ages', *Questions Vol. 5, No. 8*, Questions Publishing

Child, M. (1992) *Discovering Church Architecture*, Shire Publications, ISBN 0-85263-328-9

Coles, R. (1992) *The Spiritual Life of Children*, Harper Collins, ISBN 0-00-599310-5

Edwards, D.L. (1992) *The Cathedrals of Britain*, Pitkin, ISBN 0-85372-455-5

Soskice, J.M. (1989) *Metaphor and Religious Language*, Clarendon, ISBN 0-19-824982-9

GENERAL REFERENCES

Beavers, R.P. et al. (1988) *The World's Religions*, Lion, ISBN 0-86760-985-0

Day, D.V. et al. (ed) (1993) *The Contours of Christian Education*, McCrimmons, ISBN 0-85597-495-8

McBain, J.M. (rep. 1972) *The Book of a Thousand Poems*, Evans, ISBN 237-44328-7

Rosen, M. (1986) *The Kingfisher Book of Children's Poetry*, Kingfisher, ISBN 0-86272-155-5

(Sources for RE Practice and Theory)

Copley, T. & G. (1993) *Religious Education at Key Stage 1*, Southgate Publishers, ISBN 1-85741-046-7

Watson, B.G. (1987) *Education and Belief*, Blackwell, ISBN 0-631-15208-3

Watson, B.G. (1992) *Priorities in Religious Education*, Falmer, ISBN 0-75070-017-3

Watson, B.G. (1993) *The Effective Teaching of Religious Education*, Longman

Watson, B.G. & Ashton, E. (1994) *Education, Values & Assumptions*, Fulton, ISBN 1-85346-333-7

Copley, T. (1994) Collective Worship: An INSET Video for Schools, Southgate, ISBN 1-85741-067-X